Mercy Wears a Red Dress

Mercy Wears a Red Dress

DAVID CRAIG

RESOURCE *Publications* • Eugene, Oregon

MERCY WEARS A RED DRESS

Copyright © 2016 David Craig. All rights reserved. Except for brief quotations in critical publications or reviews, no part of this book may be reproduced in any manner without prior written permission from the publisher. Write: Permissions, Wipf and Stock Publishers, 199 W. 8th Ave., Suite 3, Eugene, OR 97401.

Resource Publications
An Imprint of Wipf and Stock Publishers
199 W. 8th Ave., Suite 3
Eugene, OR 97401

www.wipfandstock.com

PAPERBACK ISBN: 978-1-5326-0803-2
HARDCOVER ISBN: 978-1-5326-0805-6
EBOOK ISBN: 978-1-5326-0804-9

Manufactured in the U.S.A.   NOVEMBER 1, 2016

Contents

THE PAPAL SASH

We did say a rosary in the car— | 3
Advent is kind of trumped | 5
To Our Lady | 7
Sagrada Familia | 9
The Vatican | 11
I use a tiny bowl for cereal | 13
Yeats, once a raven, haystack | 15
Pat's face tints | 17
Larry fights a Rottweiler | 19
Pix's horse | 21
Grandma McElwee's Irish house | 23
My parents bought me | 25
My twelve-customer paper route | 27
Sports-ing | 29
Being a winner | 31
Sunday mornings settle in | 32
The slowest flower | 34
A line, shaken, stirred | 35

Contents

My garage indicts me | 36

Life goes on after I sin | 38

The post Confessional rise | 40

Birthday poem | 42

I found this old entry about my son | 44

When the kids were born | 47

Harry the Schnauzer | 49

Thomas Merton doesn't make the fudge— | 50

There is a hollow in winter | 51

What will make us live good lives | 53

Our Lady appears so often these days | 55

The local librarians are generous | 57

Christmas on a country road | 59

We invented chocolate milk | 61

Giving Bridget a ride to school | 63

Poem for Jack | 65

"A turtle is considered obese if it is too chubby to withdraw into its shell" | 67

The light blue, a touch of white | 69

At the West Virginia Dept. of Motor Vehicles | 70

I think the VPAA must get irked | 72

If your name is Rufus | 74

People in the third world | 76

When I finally caught up with him | 78

The first time we went over the Kovach's | 79

Whenever you think you've got someone pegged | 81

Beetle busy, the world goes on | 82

So much light green encroaches | 83

O Great Cataract, volume and vowel | 84

CONTENTS

Mercy wears a red dress | 85

HAND IN HAND

Sorrows of the Virgin Mary

After Simeon | 91
The Flight into Egypt | 92
The Loss of the Child Jesus in the Temple | 93
Mary Meets Jesus on the Way to Calvary | 94
Jesus Dies on the Cross | 96
Mary Receiving the Pierced Body | 98
The Body of Jesus is Placed in the Tomb | 100

The Seven Sorrows and Seven Joys of St. Joseph

The Doubt that is Joseph | 103
The Poverty of Jesus' Birth | 104
The Circumcision | 105
The Prophecy of Simeon | 106
The Flight into Egypt | 107
The Return from Egypt | 109
The Loss of the Child Jesus | 111

GOSPEL SONNETS

Through Beelzebub | 115
A Tree and it Fruits | 116
The Pharisee would be a Sign | 117
The Return of the Unclean Spirit | 118

ST. ANTHONY SPEAKS

The presentation made by St. Anthony to people who spoke various different languages | 121

St. Anthony preaches to the fish | 123

How he was seen simultaneously in two places | 125

St. Anthony assists a monk who was tempted sexually | 126

He replaces a woman's hair that had been torn off her head | 127

He reveals one of Satan's tricks to the friars | 129

How he boldly preached against vices | 131

How a downpour did not dampen his listeners | 132

The angelic postman | 133

Notes | 135

Acknowledgments | 139

The Papal Sash

WE DID SAY A ROSARY IN THE CAR—

that was something, though it was hard to hear
all the voices. Today I'll go to Confession,
can't say which of my lambs will follow.

"Onward Christian Soldiers" we are not,
except for Mrs. Polite, as mom calls herself
in one of Jude's programs.
And in truth, she has grown, by leaps
and bounds, while the rest of us,
I'm afraid, are more hopper types—
about the back yard, in the basement,
all over the furniture; hopping
and nibbling, nibbling.

We are still everything we aren't.

There's no brightening it:
the flag we will wave when Jesus comes back
will be a beat one. We'll probably
have to tie one of the ends in a knot
to the staff; though our waving, we hope,
won't be abashed, or too much
of an embarrassment for our neighbors.

Still, today is a new day, and there is
the Confession thing. Life does get better,
like that horrible PRINCE OF EGYPT song:
"If you believe"—though I don't think

creatively seeing makes anything happen.
Like the rest of our lives, that's too shallow,
shoddy to do much good.

This is the Valley of the Lord, east end.
The part near the river, behind the tracks.

We can clean up, comb our hair,
but there's no hiding who we are.

We are the blessed.

ADVENT IS KIND OF TRUMPED

    by the Christmas tree, though no child
    rushes to help me spread its artificial wings!
    Our Down's guy, however, does note
    repeatedly that he's on the "nice" list.
    At twenty-one, he gets his mall picture taken
    with me and Santa.

    My ADHD daughter, on the other hand,
    who does not suffer fools, or her dad, easily,
    has a heart for anything small, while our eldest,
    an Aspy, offers only jagged glimpses of his—
    bold pen and ink outlines. They are gift,
    part of that humble crowd which will lift its face
    skyward soon enough, waiting for reindeer,
    or something very like that.

    I wait for a publisher. My wife, who knows
    what she waits for? Maybe better hands
    at the piano, though she is already quite good.
    Maybe a husband who behaves as he ought.
    And the kids? For another world, no doubt,
    one to their specs. The trees wait for snow
    this time of year, the grass for frost. Snow
    is the stuff of hope because it means Christmas,
    days off; it means sledding and eggnog,
    all the family—a tree to light in the evenings!
    It's like when we used to have summer sleep-outs

in our back yard tent, listen
to THE LORD OF THE RINGS.
Nothing could've been cooler.

It's good to still have them here, despite
the edges. They are, thankfully, who they are
and where they have been.

We will try again this evening, my wife and I—
to make this their home.

TO OUR LADY

    Thanks for not pitching my garbage,
    for not letting it seek its level
    among the banana peels, Monster drink cans,
    half of New York City.

    Thank you for over-looking my failings—
    which pilgrimage like prayerful
    maggots up the insides of summer trash cans,
    across the lids: they slowly herd themselves,
    turning, tiny mouths lifted in song—
    they cannot see! But that does not stop them
    as they make their way toward a new Jerusalem.

    Thank you for smiling through your statue's paint
    when I come to visit you in Adoration—
    for liking me more than the world does.

    You are home to me, not this artfully
    messy office, 25-year consolation pen set;
    not my widescreen TV at home; not even
    football. I could cross my legs in prayer
    like a yogi if I want. It would not matter.

    You would pull the cover up under my chin
    at night, sing me a song.

    Let the world go on as it does; I will dance

around my older children, make strange noises
to amuse them. They may not understand,
but will be gathered in.

Thank you for today. Good things might
very well happen! A stranger could knock
on my door. A check could arrive,
students line the halls with lifted pens, confetti.

Someone I don't know could cut my grass.

SAGRADA FAMILIA

You could see the Mediterranean
from the towers, the colored fruit,
the script; stained glass on fire inside, high
boles on pillar trees, all the creation,
elevation, cool space prayer could use.

Gaudi was in town too, where his angels
got fined for his every over-the-top attempt
to amend the human condition.
("We need more sidewalk here.")

But it's always mercy, the people, isn't it,
who finally make a trip? The guy
who tried French to direct lost us, our
first night in Barcelona; he left, only
to come back, help us find our hostel.

Picasso and Dali showed,
but it was the other Gothic Cathedral
that spoke to Linda and me: an organist,
as if on cue, up high and to the left
beginning her Bach as we came in—
a trumpeter, my delight, soon joining in.

And the people in Gaming:
the philosopher and historian hoisting tankards,
all the families, inviting us over for dinner.

(Professor Cassidy, in kilt, leaving
that semester, calling us "the dear Craigs.")
And St. Joseph himself: the grounds man,
Maros—his family, his own Downs' son;
priests too, Fr. Matthew, on the bus,
making amends for leaving us behind
in his mad rush for Mercy's Polish shrine.

Campus children came over to sing
my shy daughter happy birthday.

St. Francis breathed Assisi, sure;
Anthony, delivering his delightfully
third-world Padua; St. Paul, inside-his-walls.

(And in Rome, when I had to pull my Down's guy,
stuck, through a moving metro door.)

Europe was, is, thankfully, not America.
It breathes a different air, less cowboy waste,
more concern for the little things, for the fact
that they are all in this together.
Post-colonialist tact perhaps. I didn't belong,
but liked the fact that they seemed to.

There's no denying it: Austrians
kill their babies, too, but they so obviously
pay for it. You can see that in how kind
and isolated they are.

Who will ever save us from ourselves?

And when will He come?

THE VATICAN

They hadn't time to sort the modern—
our Jesuit guide called it "mom's fridge."
(Besides, there was the matter of donations.)

I wanted to idiot time,
go back to the Renaissance tripe,
him noting that the painter had revised
900 times. "How many people
would do that today?"

By the time we got to the Sistine: ceiling,
walls of Marvel—comics, Thor and Captain
America's abs, I had to tell him:
they needed to get down there,
make some calls.

The best do not deserve the rest.

This was the Vatican for God's sake.

*

It was funny; though large, the whole place
stuck me as homey, small in some way:
too many statues—even the huge courtyard
out front, which had always seemed
like all of history on tv. The stones there
felt gathered from backyards everywhere,

the whole show put together on the fly.

"We don't have much money here,"
our young cleric said; and oddly enough,
that felt about right.

*

My son pointed out Cesena's donkey ears,
Michelangelo's droop: sheet of skin,
not smiling, hanging down—a four-year
penance from Julius II.

"Okay," I had to admit.
"He may have revised."

I USE A TINY BOWL FOR CEREAL

    so I don't eat too much,
    but then I have a second helping.

    This happens—so it must be metaphor:
    a human being, tying to lose what won't leave,
    trying to catch what he can't.
    Either is on point, and both better
    than the alternative, which is what happens
    when one becomes—how else to put it—
    contemporary?

    Do they hide underneath my table
    when forgotten: metaphors, I mean?
    Do they finally make peace with the Easter Bunny,
    the length of childhood? I like to think of them
    under there with the dog, at the ready,
    to play if all else fails. Or if else does not.

    They are the bulbs on my Christmas tree,
    make-up on a beautiful woman.

    They are every day you're not here!

    But even if you were, that would only
    be for a time, wouldn't it? And then
    the mundane takes over again, with all its
    little jobs and goings. And that's okay,

at least until I wake again, early,
listen to the heavenly shuffle.

I need to prepare a place for you, just in case
you arrive, and for me as well—
the one I'm happiest with.

Of course most of my days are spent
on family, making this cushion set right
for Sally, putting that train back on track
for Bill, watching the whole scene
with my wife as the sun sets,
her sipping her lemon pekoe tea.

The bells ring on the tree then,
of their own accord. But there are no movies,
no Wonderful Lifes besides this one,
which just happened
as it sometimes does.

YEATS, ONCE A RAVEN, HAYSTACK

    occasionally returns—
    not so flinty as he could be in life.
    He's up for most sport, doesn't seem
    to mind that he's not very good
    at volleyball or field hockey—or that
    it's tough to move in that suit, cravat,
    nez thing. He's happy, and being tall
    helps in all kinds of ways. Don't
    know for sure if he's onto
    the bigger road yet, but I hope so:
    mistakes are just mistakes after all,
    each gone soon enough, like the bad
    in everybody's life. I hope
    to meet him, though he'll probably
    have moved on by then.

    Maybe HD is with him, Pound as well—
    who could certainly captain any team—
    "Father and Gateway to the East."
    That had to count for something.

    HD has to work off the Freud, WC
    Williams, his sure pace; at the well,
    always, it seems, at the well.

    But I like to think that Cuchulain
    has been comforted, his shroud completed,

all these years after the mummy dance.

Most everyone you want to, I suspect,
you'll get to see over there, if you
get over the humps yourself that is.

I like to think of WB lying down
in a meadow his language helped create:
a nice blue moss interspersed, all
the trees you want. Other folk,
fans, as well, real and otherwise.
The high "e"s will offer just
the right amount of resistance
as you recline; recumbent liquids,
consonants making no end
to that repose.

Birds would lace the edges,
and you'll probably be able to hear
the sound of distant laughter. Maybe
his chords, notes, are like the future,
calling him, us. Maybe it was
always like that—nothing can take
what he's given, nor the care
with which he gave it.

And his friends, family, politicos?
They're all laughs, arms about
the shoulder now. The good
is the good, after all, and that
was what brought them to him
in the first place.

His life—a life like yours, mine,
but not at all like either;
a worthwhile stop, short or long,
on the road to more.

PAT'S FACE TINTS

    a cigarette grey. But that doesn't
    seem to slow him down. He's tended
    his machine shop for forty years, providing,
    arrives at every family get-together
    without flags or roses. Nothing, except him,
    is ever about that.

    I don't know how he does it,
    want to be like him; but it is too late.
    I have a different job and a family
    that wouldn't fit into his house.
    They would require different curtains,
    confections, their own puppy.

    So while it's true we all usually do the best
    we can; his is clearly better than mine.

    He's not the only one like that, of course.
    There are far too many of those good types
    around this Catholic University, (so many
    holy people, you can't count them)
    sandals I can't loose.

    Thankfully, they don't ask,
    or wear them, except in the summer,
    like that Orthodox Jew Linda and I met
    walking through downtown Pittsburgh

one summer eve. He thought I was
of his tribe, was collecting funds
for something holy. I had
no money, but wanted to bend down
and kiss his feet—didn't.

Some wimpery lasts forever.

Pat would understand that:
he's been in the navy—
he has this reel-to-reel with all
the golden oldies on it: "Last Kiss,"
by J. Frank Wilson, "Tammy's in Love."

Somebody like that would never lie to you.

LARRY FIGHTS A ROTTWEILER

It was something he had to do.
The thing was dragging an old woman
across his lawn by her ankle.

That would have been hard
for anyone to ignore.

He's got scars now, war wounds,
but seems happy enough—
if you don't count the personal issues.
(His wife left him, but comes back
periodically to clean.)

I had free tickets, took him once
to a Browns game, all these people
on the Rapid Transit with faces painted
orange, barking like dogs.

Must be something about the town.
We cannot win, but are legion—
though I'm thinking, too, that what
owns us might go deeper, better.
In the end, I don't think we believe
in winning; I mean,
whose life is like that?

At any rate, the two of us
were right there with the rest of them:
a deficit, all we would never become,
barking after leaves, touchdowns.

We've never really known the other,
he and I, though we are each equally
amused at his brother. I speak outrageous,
out of touch with the West Side:
wrenches, car frames, his blunt
assessment of anything near at hand.
For his part, he fishes around
for things to say: kids, beer and food.
The rest is sports teams.

I still like him though: one
of the only strangers I'll ever know,
brother to my past, blood, brother
who does what he does
because he has no home.

PIX'S HORSE

    has been left afield—though with
    or without her new teeth (a nice set),
    she's always been real as the red
    in a swirl of autumn leaves—
    is there the moment she picks up the phone.

    Her eyes wane: a mercy, perhaps,
    given how much she's seen of this world.

    Even her aneurysms sing her praise.

    There are many people like her,
    of course—the undecorated, the constant,
    amid what will defeat us all in the end.
    She could be a Quarles emblem:
    Patience, a little old woman, stooped
    at a bend in the road, waiting
    with a nice slice of pie.

    Neither she nor her hubby have jobs,
    often, but they do not change her.
    More than anyone else,
    she's given our name a house to live in.

    These days, she's usually playing poker
    when I arrive. You can watch her
    on the internet. I sometimes think

it's because we don't have much to say,
but suspect, rather, that it's
the adrenaline: little kings marching
out your door—always, in one way
or another. And who likes that?
It's worse than an empty fridge, except
for baloney spread, because you can't
get them back, or anything else really.

GRANDMA MCELWEE'S IRISH HOUSE

felt like a 50s Catholic Church:
cool, dark, reverent—large painted statues,
wavering votive candles, a sliding
Confessional screen. And doilies!
They made her polished end tables, old lamps,
seem other—like something out of Joyce.

She loved us, in earnest, quietly,
like the swish of young cassocks in a nave.
Pillow mints in small bowls graced her table;
a fine, smooth ironed white cloth beneath.

Outside, a transistor radio pressed
to my ear on her front steps, I caught
Baltimore baseball: a game from another
city! It shocked me, the want in those
announcing voices, the crowd in the stands
as well; each needing Oriole success
as much as I needed that for my own team.

How many people there must be out there
in the world. What place could I have,
make for myself? Surely there were doctors
there, a ton of scientists. Even if I learned
enough, there was the question
of perseverance. At 7, what had I ever
seen through; what could I, always
so far from any goal, achieve?

It was like walking into a library
for the first time, seeing all those books.

I would never finish them.

As I went back inside, small boy, Grandma,
always, in memory, in a black dress: I asked
her to pray for me to the woman
framed in palms fronds, St. Therese.

I could see her fret. (She said she would.)

But the thing is, I don't think
it's different for anybody. We are all
ill-equipped, not ready for anything,
not ready to be heroes. We are still
on a porch or in a dark room, a quiet radio
or a family of voices pressed like mercy—
yes—into our ears.

MY PARENTS BOUGHT ME

a tall cardboard store one Christmas,
empty labeled cans, boxes for the shelves.
It was generous; and though I liked feeling
that I might have a grocer's place
in this world—I didn't.

Did I want to sell my helpful sister
some beans? Why, yes I did!
But that was it: no conversation, no tension,
no narrative; just "You shop," "I sell."

Another possible direction—dashed!

A young Shelley
would have been good company
at that point: all the tides and empty seas
in the world—in a grey basement—
everything reduced to what was not there!

How quickly, I wonder, did that little shop
get set aside? How quickly did the cardboard
age, bend, unattended; how quickly did it,
like my parents' optimism,
find its way to the curb?

Parental silence is a horrible thing:
watching as they sift, trying to guide.

Thankfully, my position of Professor
is much easier to maintain, probably
because the narratives come to you, yes—
but then we can all be so goofy, too.
One can almost fit in without trying.
And being a poet, of course, happily
halves any expectations.

I have my little art cards
taped to my office door, my shop—less
than it should be, to nobody's concern.

MY TWELVE-CUSTOMER PAPER ROUTE

notwithstanding, order never did descend;
though one winter morning, in Kent, Ohio,
as I walked, transistor in my ear—
made in Japan!—I was struck by news:
Robert Frost had died.
In fifth grade then, I don't remember
if I even knew what poetry was; only that
this mattered, more than Skeeter Davis.

And then later, in eighth grade, high
in our dormers, reading a line from
Browning, something about a
"shroud of snow"; I stayed with it,
even as winter covered us, again, outside.
I thought I might be a poet then.

But no one could make a living at that!

Loneliness stamps us from the beginning.
When someone says "I feel lonely,"
part of me wants to laugh—–though
that's how the other world knocks, where it
comes alive, in: all the saints playing cards,
butts hanging out of their mouths,
waiting for you to clock in or take a walk
in the country; Jesus, like some
long-forgotten uncle, nodding; Mary—

who thinks the world of your company.

Dude, they say, (in a younger voice),
go back over there, take Tuesday.
And so I bend to it a-gain, on my chair, ride
it out, early in the morning, typing away
like Billy Collins, under a little porcelain
take of a Pope, a new saint, John the XXIIIrd,
who was a chain smoker,
and so the patron saint of all of us.

SPORTS-ING

When I was a kid on my 60s
high school football team, a few of us,
the slackers, would turn our coaches:
"When the going gets tough—
the smart cut out."

But as I listened to my favorite team
take the apple on the radio, I realized,
once again, how true those old
sayings are. "There is no 'I' in team."

They lost simply because they'd won
too many in a row. Sooner or later,
complacency demands to be counted
at the table. (We are talking humanity here!)

You could see it in their photographed faces:
offensive linemen, devastated—as
we all are when we fail publicly.

Rhetoric or politics don't help then.
Spin doctors can't rewrite a scoreboard.

The 'I' has left the bench—
lies fat and prone, weeping on the field.
(He delays the season, but doesn't care
about anything but his crayon tears,

the bicycle he didn't get for Christmas.)

My family is a team of sorts. How hard
do I pull when my name won't get lifted
for the fray? And the saints? My God,
they invented team, didn't they?
And no politically correct lesson
will help on that pitch. You are what
you do. I want to say that in heaven
everyone is a Reagan Republican,
but that would surely offend somebody.

There they are free because
they never thought about others enough
to judge. There's no academic ego
therapy there. There they are all the lost,
the poor—the people who can't
coordinate clothing, people with
bad shoes, unbrushed teeth, people
who listen to horrible music,
some in leather homeless helmets,
some in 50s gear, no face masks,
big numbers, with hip pads so high
that they stick up and out of the pants.

Single wing, baby. Call out some signals!
Look like you know what you're doing!
(There's only strength in numbers
if you're on the same page.)

You may not be going anywhere—
but how can you say for sure?

BEING A WINNER

I think I want to be a winner today,
though that TV, "sell me some Jesus" stuff
is out. I want to be a winner, running
through my grass; not with bare feet
because we're deep in the fall now.
Maybe I'll be a winner on my recliner.
No one else is here, except you—
but what does that matter? Winning, after all,
is a state of mind, a plaque we can place
inside somewhere; an announcement
we can make to encourage others, ourselves
when the time is right—
to fill a Shakespearean breach!

Or maybe being a winner
is sitting in the bull's eye of God, His will.

Maybe it's the long walk home, a walk
so protracted that it makes you a loser too.
Losing is so much sweeter when it's done
by a winner, by one of the ones
walking the long walk home.

SUNDAY MORNINGS SETTLE IN

early, rise slowly with the sun
over frosted grass. You can hear the heater
as it hums. Nothing is allowed to happen
on Sundays. You must learn to wait.
Sundays are like a great port near New Orleans,
without a ship in sight.

It's like a feast without food. You sit down
to table, someone else's, though you don't know
what to expect, or if anything will be served.

Fewer cars run on Sunday. You can see that
out your front window. Most just
won't turn over. Some people try to shop
on Sundays, but that doesn't work either.
Cash registers don't open, sales people disappear
almost as soon as you turn your head.

And don't ask about football. Nobody plays
on Sunday. You can't find a game anywhere,
in backyards or at the cold beach.

Every aunt, living or dead, comes to visit
on Sunday, each in her best.

Time itself does not exist on Sundays.
The illusion simply subsides, evaporates.

You can play an instrument on Sunday,
but not loudly (in Germany), and the music
must be ethereal, apace. Friends can visit
as every bit of laughter is absorbed on Sunday,
into the walls, into a pale marble-blue sky.

It's a good thing Sunday only comes once
or twice a week. It's a good thing that
someone else is responsible for reconstructing
time after it subsides. We might walk
right out of our shoes were it otherwise.
There would be no heaven, no earth.
There would be no bustle. We would
simply cease to exist as we know it.

I'm not sure if that would be a good thing
or not. But such are the limitations of time.

THE SLOWEST FLOWER

is humility, which begins,
like every mind, to unbind:
more slowly
than one would have thought possible.

People are sometimes
happy with that.

A LINE, SHAKEN, STIRRED

    by what slight wind, little bird?
    By what—green? Summer is long gone.
    The trees are bare, grey, give back
    nature's surprise. Our lives are like that,
    best when bare, under snow. And the fields,
    what of them in this stiffer wind, this more
    demanding sun? (Though maybe not of you.)

    Mary is the kindest, that is why
    she's so blessed. Francis too, Thérèse, Faustina,
    all of them. Who else has been so good to you,
    through your ups and downs? Who else
    has walked with you these miles—
    in robe and sandal? Who else understands
    the seasons, the reasons why we must change?

    We cannot repay them, these elven
    folk, these citizens of the far place.

    But that is not why they come.

MY GARAGE INDICTS ME

in these rows of small cob-webby jars:
screws, left-overs from the previous owner,
nine years gone. And now my wife
buys a new variable speed drill set.
Make no mistake, I'll have to use the thing—.

Screws are easy, you can see the threads,
just have to follow; but what about
the rest of my house? I still don't know
how to turn on the artificial fireplace,
how to program the thermostat,
or how to change the furnace's filter. ("Oh,
you don't know that either?" "No, I don't.")

The good thing about teaching is that
we have only 26 identifiable letters.
You can mix, match, teach students how
they can be configured and to what end.

I'm grateful they pay me for this,
and for the fact that I can still put my own
pants on, (another poem there) tie a tie,
boil a hot dog. But that's about it.
That's always been it.

When I was a kid, I tried to run my brother,
Tim's, train. You had this button

in your hand, had to slow its speed for turns.
But I couldn't: too much pressure. What
if I got it wrong? (And I would too.)
So the thing ran off the track every time.
The same thing later on his motorcycle:
one down, three up, something like that.
Nah, first gear all the way—until
he chased me off the thing.

And how am I going to teach
my banjo teacher about this? How am I
going to learn when each step forward
calls to two steps back, each mistake
issuing a citation I seem to need.

And how in God's holy name
have I gotten this far?

LIFE GOES ON AFTER I SIN

which is a blessing to me. No one stops,
gets off the bus, no one lobbies
for my removal. It's kind of reassuring.
It's like Jesus is saying, "There are lots
of stupid people here. You fit right in.
Don't worry." After all, you never really know
about them—those others—do you?
Though of course we would not wish that
on (almost) anyone. There, I'm doing it again.
I close my eyes, wait; again, nothing.
Destruction averted.

It hasn't snowed yet, at least not here;
and my three-card solitaire game is still intact.
Car still runs, I still have a job and a family
that are none the wiser—nor have they
ever been. Damn—darn. Three, four strikes
as I unclench. I like the keeper of the keys here
as I ask for forgiveness again.
It's like being a kid at Christmas. Who knows
which of those packages are for you?
This one's a Monday, this, a Tuesday.
This one is the student who, though nice,
doesn't like to feel criticized.

And so I dance inside. You cannot
reach me because I cannot defeat myself.

I have a Dad, big and strong. He has planted
his flag next to me and will not be moved.
No matter how hard I try!
(And I don't want Him to.)

I feel like a garden, newly planted.
I feel like a Met in 1969.

I can sing la la all I want because the soil
is good here, because I like the fence.

THE POST CONFESSIONAL RISE

New chances are good.

Even the outside of the mall looks great
this evening, under a late sunset, orange clouds—
or maybe stars are overhead by now:
the lights, the cars, Christmas down the line.
Walmart looks like an oasis, a grade school friend.

All of them, gone. None will read this.
Most came to girls quicker, left by college,
my first leg of it anyway. It always
struck me as odd, how when I'd meet them later,
they'd always seem to expect the same guy—
as if human experience stopped at fifteen.
You had to wonder, had it been so for them?

Still, I miss the old baseball mitts:
those players, those days. We were as alike
as the era would allow: Beatles and Rolling Stones
kids, never quite out of school,
fast to the new, slow to anything that mattered.

Brothers, I salute you—most Appalachian
transplants, as I was, though I hadn't
learned that yet. If I could see them again,
I would: Danny Keeney, David Dorton,
my baseball buds, fastballs in a world
built for better players, bigger diamonds.

We all run our course, and if we're lucky,
we meet all kinds of people along the way—
some worth their weight in memory:
for their sustained lack of discretion,
because it made the time worth our lives.

BIRTHDAY POEM

She has given the years,
poured them out on the ground
right in front of me, like some fine
oyster Hollandaise, Béarnaise,
cabbage soup.

Always other, her side is
gadgets, electrical switches, and comfort:
after-the-Depression style.
They value what they can see.

I can count the ways we are,
thankfully, not one. Some of them
grow! (Who would want
duplicates running around, echoing
your every presentiment?)

Her wounds keep us real,
as deep as the rivers beneath rivers;
some of them—we will thankfully
say—were never quite healed.

This is how you know you are home!

Having spent a long time here,
the two of us know that there is
no good that does not have a name,

that does not come out of this ground.
There is no good that does not
wear a watch.

Unpolished, she is all wit,
metaphysical wiggle, piano lessons,
odd lunches—kale and egg, vegetable
hair, blueberries and walnuts.

(Even if we have too much furniture.)

She is entirely herself, cannot
be moved, even when she is.

It's the oldest dance—we lift a foot,
"signifying matrimonie . . . which
betokeneth," as every husband knows,
"concorde."

I FOUND THIS OLD ENTRY ABOUT MY SON

in bed with an over-sized Piglet, arm draped
over the thing, sweaty head hidden: strep.
Apparently, I'd peered under the substantial
pink ear to see his eyes—wrapped in sickness.
He did not plead, but was stuck,
good to see his dad.

And I think of my own mother, pacing
at the foot of my bed, clearly realizing
that there was nothing she could do,
either for my illness, or for my plight.

Years later she'd say:
"I don't know if he has what it takes
to make it in this world."

(Why get on the playground round-about?
"It just keeps going in circles.")

She knew I was too concerned
with every wrong, stuck on the first one.

There was nothing she, grieving, could do,
as I tried to keep the thermometer in place.

(She certainly didn't trust my father's
Jansenistic glee at my First Communion:
me all shiny and clean in my first suit,

affirmed by heaven and earth: the tie,
the straight fold of the hands. She disliked
the Irish squeeze: probably wanted some light,
success, a little Protestant money.

She wanted, like the rest of us,
a God with sunny beaches.)

My son is still sick, though,
back there in the past—nothing I can do
for him either. (I hope I stroked his brow,
kissed him, thanked him for being so brave.)

And now, later: a grown man, an Aspy's
in his parents' basement, frustrated
by his stuck, looking for a career to stamp him.

If I could make paper cranes I would;
I'd put two on his basement table, one
on either side of his computer. I'd fly
a few around the ping-pong table
for his amusement.

I would read Chinese poetry aloud,
the Rexroth translations, but that
would not help. No, life is lonely.
Ask Basho. That's why our mothers
always tried to feed us too much.

He will, mercifully, move past this.
We all do. And there will be a future for him,
whether he comes upon it, or it upon him.
And there will be a woman somewhere,
as fine as his own mother. She will help,
offer her wounds to help him grow,
just as he will offer his.

I raise my glass: Mr. Bringer-of-the-New,
My-Heart-Who–Walks-Away-from-Me—
as he always has, in a fine stride.

WHEN THE KIDS WERE BORN

    I slept in an old bowling shoe: a chair
    next to my wife's hospital bed.

    After that things got better.
    Like now, at the library, where Down's Jude
    is the only kid here for Karaoke night,
    and so wins all the prizes—

    though those songs! (Dads knows
    the price of parenthood: the car radio.)
    Love for the young, apparently,
    is an extended shudder. Their declarations,
    worth what exactly?

    Linda has a better take—says it's youth,
    spring, the generosity of Christ: flowers
    so full of themselves
    that they flush at their own color.

    We haven't seen our kids' mates:
    as far as we know—one of my students
    in Austria, standing hopefully next to David
    at the wee-hours Polish bus stop.
    Slightly nerdy, gifted—but a prettier,
    more talkative young woman took up the time.

    They say age has its recompense,

but I don't know that I've seen it.
Who is more foolish than an old person,
still clinging to the wrong things,
tented under faded wallpaper
that won't adhere—though that
is a mercy, too. It helps kids with error,
provides a human backdrop.
We know something about life, after all,
about bad choices—and we don't
mind listening.

HARRY THE SCHNAUZER

The family dog remembers Verdun,
would take the last bullet. He's survived
wet, frozen trenches, the machine gun,
yellow snowflake, the curl of mustard gas.
(He would give up a large bone
for a patch over his left eye.)

Picked up by family, flattened
on his back in someone's arms,
he is still a soldier, accepts his fate,
a mutiny only the hero would understand.

When he walks he is Leaf-beard:
all business, the other dogs (ladies
of the leash) can have their skips, their
yappy biscuit shows, he is concerned
with the safety of the neighborhood.
He knows that changes always begin locally.
He knows the power of the vote.

THOMAS MERTON DOESN'T MAKE THE FUDGE—

probably because he has better things to do,
though I can't imagine what.
The saved have been so, and those on the road
probably don't need him much any more.

Would it be such a stretch
to see walnut bourbon fudge as one of those places
where heaven becomes earth, where the Church
needs to call in the Dominicans
to make the proper distinctions—
though everyone knows they sneak.

Jesus, for his part, takes on a younger form,
licks the spoon. Even the urgently home-schooled
come around.

Heaven—one big kitchen.

Maybe no prayers get answered on this day.
Maybe the great sigh comes early, just this once,
every old-town gothic cathedral,
its bells, standing down.

Angels can put their feet up.

It's not so much that Christmas has come early.
Rather, it has never left, again.

$27.95 is not so much to pay.

THERE IS A HOLLOW IN WINTER

a bear in a tree, not to mention wolves,
padding through forests to the north of us—
arranging, deepening night. But this
is southern Ontario, and I am grumbling
my way across the Madonna House compound,
its sparkling white shoulders, paths,
toward a lit dining room.

Part of me doesn't want to go in—
would rather walk my way into the wilderness.
Some young lady, you see, hasn't adequately
returned my hello!

These days, I try to remember that feelings
are friends—though I'd like to know who
decided that? It's like when sports commentators
say, "It's all good." Tell that to Robert Frost
when he cuts off most of your hand, leaves you
waving it there like a bloody flag, as you try
to turn the page, keep it clean.

No, it's not all good. I mean, who looks forward
to death? Not the finished product, you on a slab;
no, that's the easy part. I'm talking about
the winnowing: when your aperture
begins to narrow, when you start to panic,
losing all you know of yourself?

Yes, line us up.

Of course, it's times like this that the Bible,
as most good answers, waits with an other-worldly
calm, patience. Not obtrusively—but opened
on a table, in smooth pages, like a dear friend,
some red ink or gilded edges to draw you in.

If it were a kid's book, movie, it would
do that literally. You could live for awhile
among floating words, letters. If interactive,
you could change characters, endings.
You could paint with the brush of your choice,
be edified, every step of the way.

But this is not a kid's story, and so you
must wait—in the wait, if you know
what I mean, like everybody else in line:
some smoking, some looking off in the distance.

Offer a mint, a timely quip.
What else can you do?

WHAT WILL MAKE US LIVE GOOD LIVES

–for Wayne Lewis

if He has not. What will make us new
if we won't be? What mercy can take us
if we insist on delay?

One deeper than we know:
for there is a mercy that moves mountains,
that is moving them now. If you
cannot feel it, that is probably because, as yet,
you cannot feel.

Learn to be quiet, then, (I say to myself)
learn to attend, which means
"to stretch after."

This is what Advent is for.

*

And so I wait for the smallest things,
what will truly change me:
a doorbell, perhaps, a football game
at a friend's house.

I have no name—
except the one he gives me.

Perhaps that's why
God might have so little to say
on judgment day.

OUR LADY APPEARS SO OFTEN THESE DAYS

    perhaps we should set a place for her
    at our table—if she were to so grace us, I mean.
    We could find out what they eat in Nazareth.
    I don't know if she likes poetry, but I
    could read, not my own stuff—or exclusively so.
    Linda and I could walk her around our block
    like we did for Franz and Liz Wright;
    but who knows what her agenda would be?
    So we'd have to be flexible, accommodating.
    I hope she won't be staying with others
    at the same time, not in the neighborhood, I mean.
    We could meet her again on our walk.
    And then what would we say? I wonder,
    does she come more often near Christmas?
    Will there be the faint smell of hay?
    Will Joseph wait outside, distant, like in crèches?
    (I suppose traditions must be observed.)

    She would no doubt bring gifts for the kids,
    no matter how old they are, maybe a book
    for me. I might sneak a peak at the title, but
    I hope not rudely so. (It would say so much.)

    What would I ask her I wonder?
    What would I be pressed to know?
    And how could I stay on my knees
    even after I initially rise? But that

might be why she comes: to teach me how
to eat and breathe, how to move
and have my being.

Red Dwarfs could come after that,
the sound of water—running all of summer.
I could ask her to re-circuit my head,
to fix Guatemala. But I suspect I will be asked
to just stand there, to wait until I know
what to do—and then do that.

THE LOCAL LIBRARIANS ARE GENEROUS

know us by our names. All our "holds"
sit shelved together in the back.

The sky outside is clear and dark;
it's cold for the first time this year.

I do not know what's coming.
I'm not even sure what's here, beyond
the lights, the lined blacktop, Lowe's
hardware store down the hill.
They say angels will descend, that
the veil between this world and the next
will be torn, that nobody will be the same.

That would be a good thing, surely.

Arabs and Jews, lions and lambs,
terrorists and everybody.

What would they look like, I wonder?
Would they throw down their guns,
heads with an "Aw shucks"—
or would they forget even that?
Maybe they'll get so caught up in the sky,
the angels, the Son of Man,
that earlier versions of them
will just dissolve into the night air.

Of course, there's always the matter
of accountability, but who of us
can hope to stand? No, I think
we'll take our neighbors as they come,
happy just to still be taking air.

CHRISTMAS ON A COUNTY ROAD

Each spindly grey tree reaches
in a twisted cursive—scratching
its unique space in air. What scale is this?
Nothing living belongs to The Ford Motor
Ford Company any more—ever did;
each branch is like a new kid at school,
adapting, turning through his knotted way
into something altogether new.

It's like my hand, moving: fingers—
a choreography! In tiny feathers
or a very old movie about the Congo.

And so this poem, as it turns out,
has been about Africa: Jesuit to the world!

Who is like her? Who has suffered
as she has? Up the hill, years after Europe
has gone to bed. She has borne the beating
calloused chalk-white heart
of slave-runners, mock religion.

A young black woman, Africa
gathers herself, sits on a savannah,
smoking a clay pipe, meditations rising
like her children's dreams:
some saints, some tin-pot emperors.

So it's the cordiality of the moment
that matters to her—amid the banging
metal lockers downtown at the gym.
A new single mom, she feels it, how
everything just seems to work against her
on some days: Abidemi won't do
his homework, Azubuike
wipes out a village.

She would cry out for help,
but what other continent would hear?

WE INVENTED CHOCOLATE MILK

and air hockey. So anything is possible.
The moon might be next.
And if peace on earth seems beyond us,
perhaps we could uninvent the tank.

That would solve so many problems—
a few well-placed changes.
There'd be more faces in the world!

Or not.

And so here we are again, left with a riddle,
choking an enigma—us.

Maybe we could start over,
take new names! James. It's simple,
Biblical. People named James always
get it right—and so probably
for all the wrong reasons. Maybe
we shouldn't even have names. That
would certainly make for more eye contact,
fewer possessions. (Our clothes,
dishes could make rounds, take on lives
of their own.)

But I wouldn't go further than that.
I like existing a good 90% of the time:

all the stars come out; it's like each
did so just for you. You can claim one, too,
buy in if you want a name.
But on most days, I don't need to go that far.
Just hanging out underneath is enough,
walking the dog as he urgently sniffs
the calligraphy of grass—
the great cartwheel of stars.

Why do we always want more?

GIVING BRIDGET A RIDE TO SCHOOL

    Linda was trying to remember
    if her mother had ever thought of doing that—
    so my brother came to mind: my preppy
    Jesuit high school, Larry's beater brakes
    giving out right there on 30th.
    He had to ram the edge of the curve
    repeatedly, work to ease us in.

    Tim, on the other hand, used wooden blocks
    to prop up his '57 Chevy's suspension.
    Coolest car in its day—until we hit a pothole;
    and then we'd have to jack the thing up, again.

    To the rich kids' credit, they were okay
    most days. You were who you were,
    and they had the sense to give you room.
    The Jesuits did a nice job, too—
    all things considered. No shootings,
    hazing; just prolonged academic panic, at least
    for an ADHD kid, before he could claim
    that name (which is my excuse
    if any of them read this).

    There were so many good teachers:
    Mr. Schmidt, Fr. Streicher, a lot of good faces
    I don't see anymore. Too close a look,
    though, reveals the sustained embarrassment

my life has been: cheating, behavioral urks.
So much to repent of.
And it didn't stop there: college, and then
more college; bad jobs, the occasional good.

We'd all like to do better in life.

Failure is the tattered robe we wear, knowingly
or not: arms lifted horizontally, in a preen—
small-time kings, queens.

It is what saves us. We are what we cannot fix.

He may touch that at some point, make us new.
But now is not the time for that.

POEM FOR JACK

Friends for forty-five years—"hip sincerity,"
is how I'd put it: loves boxing, blind dogs;
he and Marian used to offer space whenever I'd come
to New York. He at Columbia, me, on the lamb—
from lives not worth the time they demanded:
Dave Van Ronk, the Village, Angler Bar.

Religion usually creates the schism—
it hits him, I think, how bizarre my being Catholic
actually makes me.

Months pass, maybe a year, and then
I'll see him again. And it's like no time has gone—
nothing escaping commentary, excoriation.

I remember breaking down once in his car,
just after high school. (We were at the lakeshore
for a friendly game of softball—my creaking
self-consciousness had taken over,
made movement, real emotion impossible.)

Later he said that it hadn't seemed like much.

Friends are a rare air to breathe, for however
long they're around. There's a fire in the boiler
then! Any setting will do, the Medina
County Library, The House of Blues.

I've often wondered why secular liberals
make the best friends, maybe
because they have less turf to protect.

They are like glorious bits of feed to a hungry bird.

You take what you can get.

"A TURTLE IS CONSIDERED OBESE IF IT IS TOO CHUBBY TO WITHDRAW INTO ITS SHELL"

"Google fat turtles," Bridget asks
before school—and I get myself!
Here on my writing chair, I only
meet the world when it intrudes.
And why not? Turtles are who they are, after all;
what else would you expect of them?
Which is why, incidentally, they grouse
like they do, shredding into lettuce,
grumbling about Sartre or the scratches
on their clear plastic walls. He didn't
ask to be born, or borne away like this:
some pet's pet—the same rocky
configuration each day,
the exotic little waterfall.

What do I get from the deal: food, attention;
some, not enough. I get to sit here,
in my cage, harrumphing, stretching at
the neck, turning on the tiny TV remote
with my stubby web-footed hand,
not an ottoman in sight.

They do not think we can think,
here in Plato's cave: Promethean,
after Shelly; they cannot appreciate
the august turn of a prophetic head—
my *Confessions*.

My cities will unnerve them.

(I will not roll over.
I will not nose the ball.)

Oh!—a slice of pear!

Well, projects can wait, simmer.
Dinner is a fitting time to muse, to count
the ceiling holes above the Albert Hall.

This is how the great work gets done.

For Jerusalem's sake I will not be quiet.

THE LIGHT BLUE, A TOUCH OF WHITE

    bare tree, high in the early morning
    second story office window. It's pleasant,
    a new day! I will meet students in about an hour,
    say "hi" to faculty I pass in the hall, few of whom
    are actual friends—which is just as well,
    since this in not a living place. It's a
    passing through place,
    and so I have been these last 28 years.

    I'm not anxious for its transitory end,
    maybe because it's such a good metaphor:
    you give what you can, then ship out again
    to a more substantial post—home.

AT THE WEST VIRGINIA DEPT. OF MOTOR VEHICLES

counter guy asks: "Unemployed?"
though the question has nothing to do
with why I'm here.

This happens when I take tests too.
A perplexed facilitator will say,
"You know you did really well here."

It's a blessing, one I wish
I could live down to, because who of us
is anywhere close to being what he should?

I think of Flannery O'Connor on crutches
in Georgia, her fictional southern Grandma,
the one who could've had a life
had someone been there to shoot her
every minute.

We're just that thick.

I'd like to be one of the meek, to acquiesce:
a St. Francis at every turn, so small that
each remark flies over my head.
I could recline there, Hobbit-sized, and soon
the stars and every fine night would come.
There would be other little people as well,
but I might not feel the need to examine their pots,

their fine leather or bead work beneath high breezes,
the slight ache that shakes the moon, elven trees.
(You might not get the change you want
at the store in this mode, but you won't care.)

What days will be like those: self-regard,
shelved, enmeshed in a history of cobwebs?
Rodeo round-ups every week-end;
a whole parish of people who don't care
about nothing 'cept the garnish
on your latest story.

I THINK THE VPAA MUST GET IRKED

at me, mute to faculty governance.
But, I want to tell him, sustained inactivity
is part of my job description. Beaver-busy
interaction, plant-wide problem-solving
fall wide on the marge.

You have my respect, sir—
and my distance. One has to be very quiet
to hear the male bee buzz, the flower open;
one has to carefully watch his children's
mouths when they speak
to know what they are truly saying.

I'm sure your presence helps—
but not so much your public words.

You idea folk fizz around
like roman candles in meetings: articulate,
good-willed. Your children must be
the world's smallest warriors, able to take on
even that French bastard, ennui
(if they have the time).

So, please, do say hello to the other
busies, to that fellow over in accounting
who seems to think he's Marcus Aurelius.
For me it's the rigors of the hammock,

the creaking porch; my wife wringing her hands
on her apron, having just given me
a glass of grapefruit juice.

IF YOUR NAME IS RUFUS

      don't read this. People named Rufus
      have long, red ZZ Top beards, come from places
      like Pittsburgh or Sewickley; they invent new
      social programs, color-code them; they gather
      for conventions, but have them in places
      like Dubuque to avoid detection. They vacation
      in Labrador with their large families,
      tents, badminton nets.

      People named Rufus do videos on You Tube
      about the funny things pit bulls can do.
      They don't like poetry. People named Rufus
      live two blocks over, always.
      They only eat chicken and drive Volvo
      pick-ups with stickers on the back:
      "Hooray for Missy's Dance class,"
      "My kid can't spell," that kind of thing.
      People named Rufus like opera
      and walk down the middle of the road.
      They throw old mattresses down by the river
      when they think no one is looking. People
      named Rufus run for mayor, always win.

      People named Rufus laugh the loudest
      at office parties. They insist on their own
      unidentifiable music. People named Rufus
      have taken over the internet, invented it

in the first place. People named Rufus
are social prophets; they see recurring visuals
in their dreams. These show up later
in jeans commercials, ads for cologne.

People named Rufus are taking over. One
will marry your daughter. Another will change
your will. There'll be whole retirement
communities named Rufus, but you won't care
by then because you will have made peace
with the whole passing through thing.

PEOPLE IN THE THIRD WORLD

wouldn't use these little packets of soap
in their dishwasher, wouldn't have
one. And the soap might destroy their rivers—
or was that the old kind—which, incidentally,
belong to everybody else, especially after
we've destroyed our own, because we have
the power to care as much as we do.

There's no end to this kind of charity,
which is just an excuse to provide me
with distance from the real problem—
from Jesus who starves, reflected
in Hollywood's tears.

And what about the clothes I wear,
my car? Little mice could push it to save
the earth; but I'm diverting again, from
the ravages of bloated need, from the vice
and squeeze of white privilege.

What will I have for lunch, dinner?
Do I eat only what drops from trees?

We have too many shoes around our house.
We eat too much food, most of us, fat,
buffered. I'd like to make a difference—
which is another diversion,
turns the future into a prize.

And what about the people I meet today,
how will I treat them—though that too
avoids what skin and bones third-world
people actually have left, the persistent tv
flies which seem to want to lay eggs
along their wet eyes.

I should fast until Tuesday—at least;
but that always gives me a headache.
(I never make it nearly that far.)

It's good to feel uncomfortable about
these things, though that's
a complacent way to put it.

(Perhaps I could fashion a miter
before I go, in case I need to improvise.)

There is no way to end this poem.

WHEN I FINALLY CAUGHT UP WITH HIM

Bill was wearing one of those clear oxygen feeds.
The thing disturbed, looked alien, as if it were
a parasite sprouting from his nose—
though he could still go on about the verifiable origins
of the universe, his favorite tavern, a seat for his cylinder.

This is how life is: you go through, pretty much
doing what you've always done, until
you can't do it anymore. It's heroic, because
when it's all over, this is the life you've chosen,
that chose you.

It fits like an old suit. Most people walk around
more or less in God's will, there without reward, balloons.
You become the latest book you've read, the labored
daily walk to the mailbox, a wake of people behind you—
most grateful to have had the opportunity.

He is the flag he waves, doesn't know it,
a private in an army of them.

This is the life, well-lived, the apple that upsets the cart:
who knows how many Bills, playing it out—sometimes
on a quiet suburban street.

THE FIRST TIME WE WENT OVER THE KOVACH'S

Ed broke out a 2 liter cola, seventeen years old.
(No fizz.) Both he and Martha are hoarders,
the dearest Charismatics money can't buy.
When they open their home to you,
you know it's them because not one pillow
has been reset; their dining room, stuffed
with pictures, mismatched plates, chairs—
can't help but measure your own.

Whenever I run into him in the halls,
his glasses are always so smudged I wonder
how he can see. And that green water in
his office aquarium—it that right?

Better than you are.

We used to work out together.
He said he'd been a "butterball" when young,
and right away I knew he'd grown up
on a different planet.
Probably a better one.

Some people are you know, you learn
that as you get older—though that's only
revealed in oddities. The best could never
see themselves as models, which is how
you know you are on holy ground—
the kind you can make fun of.

I sometimes wish there were more than one Ed,
but the truth is, one is plenty. He's studying
to be a deacon, which—if that doesn't turn him—
will be good for the Church.

WHENEVER YOU THINK YOU'VE GOT SOMEONE PEGGED

    they go and make a fool out of you,
    start up a Habitat for Humanity
    or cure the mange.

    What's the point of being right, anyway?
    I might as well start reading movie magazines
    like the sighing lady who sat next to me
    on the Pittsburgh plane, or the earlier one,
    a shaman who said she would fast for two weeks,
    make a vision quest. (She knew too much as well.)

    Ignorance, on the other hand, is incremental;
    hard to catch because he keeps wandering off,
    losing his face to the flowers. He might be
    autistic, I can't be sure, two hands
    pressing down, again and again, into mud.

    Perhaps he will fashion a bird or an idea—
    but what's that to you?

    No, the streetlights come on soon enough;
    the stars are a thousand little people.
    Each knew Abraham. There is a place for you—
    but you will never find it.

BEETLE BUSY, THE WORLD GOES ON

like it has its own agenda: so many machinations,
the little feet, clampy jaws. It will
eat me one day. My bones will cake a cliff
or restore an ocean. Who says I do no good here?

We eat sandwiches, even when we don't:
old bones, skulls in the mayo. It's like a big party
no one gets invited to. The last round up
which never ends. We are spectators, speculators.

But my soul—my soul is an apricot!
My soul belongs to no one but summer's night air.
It raises me past grain elevators, all of Kansas.
It surfaces where it needs to, feeds ducks.

Come, animate with me. We will be like a chorus,
filaments swaying in light rain. We will change
the world because we give it movement. We make it move.

We are like half-filled glasses of God, spoons,
tones as we take this side of the street—
not for the keeping, but for the giving.

The wind blows through us here, far from celebrity.
We are bread for the birds.

SO MUCH LIGHT GREEN ENCROACHES

swarming back roads. Bicycles will be next.
Every person, a late spring flower. There will be
swimming pools and lemonade stands,
neighbors talking outside in the evening.

The truth is we could never live there, never have,
not really. Bicycles were invented by Martians,
the 50s. Even the people: pure Hollywood.

(Our '55 Ford wagon was stinging hot inside,
eight sweaty little bodies, incubators
for the world we inherited.)

Walker Percy knew this.

Where there is no need, there is no God.
Where there is no hole, the hole
becomes *Father Knows Best*.

We are a cry for Him. It's that simple, either that
or a lie which offers only comfort, can't.

We are wounds.

O GREAT CATARACT, VOLUME AND VOWEL

    You are the words you choose—.
    All praise and glory is Your phonebook:
    every tree and pencil made.

    Who could say no to these veils of mist,
    the heavy, fetid air, living banks?

    This is why the poor are so generous;
    this is why Charlie Chaplin
    had to invent himself: the last everyman—
    rickety beds, remnant walls . . . .

    They know that food and favor
    disappear long before people do,
    can laugh without teeth enough
    to cover their smiles. They always have time
    for you—if you're real enough.

    The poor are Your trumpet, Lord:
    circumspect—they hardly matter at all,
    which is to say
    they are the only door to heaven.

MERCY WEARS A RED DRESS

    sits as best she can around the campfire.
    She stutters, is never any trouble. Her name
    could be Ruth or Gladys. Mercy goes
    to Mass daily—does not ask which kind.
    The Eucharistic prayers are words made fresh
    to her, so, once houseled, she settles
    as nearly as she can, in—next to migrants,
    more borders than she can count.

    No one knows where she lives.

    You could be out chopping wood, and there
    she'll be, smiling at you from among the tress,
    for just a moment, hands fluttering like birds—
    and then they're up from several lakes. Mercy
    has dark eyes, braided hair, could be Ottawa.
    Daniel Boone was her friend.

    Mercy weeps in the Soviet Union, long after
    it's gone. She bears up under détente. Mercy
    could make maps, policy, but no one asks,
    in part because she sells cookies at the airport,
    sets up a card table next to orange-rockers,
    finger cymbals—those lovely
    Hare Krishna people.

    Mercy has many hands—fewer feet.

She lives on Scovill Ave. in Cleveland.
Her children play, unattended, by an opened
fire hydrant; a squealing, happy black confusion,
in and out of barreling water. St. Faustina
lived there in the 30s, Nazis banging
on her Ohio door. She could have gotten up,
responded, but Roosevelt, answerless,
was on the radio.

Either one would do.

Mercy is the ear we hear with,
it's all we know.

Hand in Hand

The Seven Sorrows of the Virgin Mary

AFTER SIMEON

—Luke 2: 25–35

"No king has ever calmed these waters. No prophet
leaves trouble behind. This world is way-station—collapse.

"The higher You rise, small One, the greater
will be your fall, because the lost are who You need,
and they will not follow willingly, nor for long.

"This world spells Your name now, too. It is my blood
that moves in you, the blood of all the unworthy.
You come for those who've traded a goodness
they can no longer claim for a guilt that cannot salve."

And then, more, what would happen—does for her:
"Oh, crushing of bone, the road You become!

"Whatever is coming will take us all.

"All these people: the great, the noble; it will ruin them,
me—because it will take You first. Nothing will ever
be the same, in the shallows, nor in the deeps, least of all
You, my issue, my increase.

"Whatever happens, it will break You, like firewood,
popping in the hearth, even as You allow it, watch.

"I must come along."

THE FLIGHT INTO EGYPT

—Matthew 2: 13–15

"Already.

The good God is a stone on some days, will not be moved.
He does not ask, nor console."

And soon the three of them are out the door: her,
the witness, the Universe. "I curl Him, myself, on another
Mr. Ears: grainy excoriations, the wind, Joseph's head
turned in a foreign land—as it has always been.

"Who knows what we leave behind: death, others intercepting
evil—in our places. But who? Other babes? Markless mothers?
Will it be our follower always, this snarl, wherever we go?
How many must die so that what He brings can live?

"Death is like sand along the sea."

She knows people will not stop sluicing the glass, almost human.
And so her baby squalls, her own eyes burn.

The three of them are all people. All of time.

And this new land, more foreign than the old, older than her kin,
it will be changed, in a way that will be beyond her; every soul
will know that: those who accept the pain, and those who don't.

She will be torn apart.

THE LOSS OF THE CHILD JESUS IN THE TEMPLE

—Luke 2: 41–52

Nothing surprises her.

"Public now. I've never liked this: the knowers, the known,
bustling after places they cannot possess."

The crowd is her solace: its shove, surge. It's where she belongs.
But Him—already looked to, each answer part of a larger revelation,
each question driving them closer to what is beyond them:
what will indict them, seal His fate.

They do not listen, not really, won't.

She knows that His shine will only hold them until the answers
begin to hurt. Then they'll have to move on. But they'll come back,
or versions of them, and harder, because Truth won't move. They
will be drawn like moths, each time naming themselves as something.

They will have to kill Him because He bows to no one,
because His gaze encloses everything—remakes her.

There is a question in Him as He watches her scurrying behind,
picking up clothes.

"I am all his. He knows that.

But we are alone."

MARY MEETS JESUS ON THE WAY TO CALVARY

His face now, the color of glass: razed, taken by this world—
He is everyone He's ever seen; the shake of pebbles,
walls collapsing, becoming holy writ.

There are no mercies left.

His flesh hangs like it doesn't belong. Teeth, she sees, cracked, soiled.
So many faces, not a face among them.

She must've been walking, because, for a moment,
He'd taken her, as He always had, into his gaze,
where neither love nor loneliness apologizes.

Had He said something? She doesn't remember because
He is far away again, dying to her as He always has in public.
How could she have been expected to deal with that?
A son who is never altogether here, or even when He is,
it's in a here only He can create, understand.

She wants to die away from these people, in a rain
that never comes—because His life is not for her, has never been.

The whole country laughs. Strips of skin, gobbets of blood.

He pushes her past the edges of fear, then asks for more—
more reign than she can control.

The people drive Him, as if He were breakfast.
She walks behind, ranging, because she still has legs.

This is a Mary she has never known.

JESUS DIES ON THE CROSS

—Matthew 27: 45–54

This sun was too many hands, but then the day clouded over,
thankfully, which was only right.

(She hears a hinge, back and forth, back and forth.)
Is her mind being taken?

Jesus is speaking from another world, one which formed this,
though His shape is His alone—as had always been the case.
His heart too.

All the world's a stage, without her—as every mother knows.
Her loneliness, giving wires to the sun.

Light does that.

But now He is darkness too. (She had been waiting for that.)
He is a feast for the knowers, who can fool others, if not themselves.
Oh, they poke; she's seen that, make others bleed
because they have to see the blood, that the other is real.
That is all they have. But Him, what did we ever have?

Quiet evenings. The two of them could walk, listen
to their ancestors, ages rolling in the trees.

But that was not this. Yes, He is dead. You can hear that, again.
"Did you think your cries would bring Him back?"

The dead, the only ones who can use Him now.

The nice soldier should take Him down. He is done,
though those shouting do not know that yet. Her too.
They could flay her as well. But she knows they won't—
because she is a woman. Yes, that's true: a backdrop, a field of flowers,
a rock garden. Something useful once.

Take Him down, she wants to say.

She will eat Him, food for her alone.

MARY RECEIVING THE PIERCED BODY

In this version, His last wound is a comma, no
boundary: a bloodless mouth, closing, opening its hole;
all the answers she never got, moving, deriding—
though this response wasn't her speaking.

He was dead now, you could see that; she'd fill out a paper.
Cash upon delivery. "Keep Him for as long as you like."

She wanted to rock Him. It was a song they used to sing,
the two of them, when they were younger and had hearts like grass.
"Let me take you, and me, to the shores of Galilee!"

It didn't go like that—though it might have.

He was the good every mother sees: the sail on the water—
the law, writing itself. He was Spirit and Truth, or rather,
He is, though this wound was the only place where
He could breathe now.

Just because He was dead didn't mean He was gone.

He turned bread to stone, once, because it didn't feed them—
not enough. He knew what they wanted and so went back
to the hills from which they came. Perhaps to give them this.
All the change He brought—brought nothing. Not yet anyway.

Now that He's dead, though, things will change. They
have to. He had to go there first. You can see that,

can't you? Down there—into his death, into Lazarus.
We will sit here in that world, He and I, until it's time.

That will be His time too. So I spread my tunic out
over my lap, the way I used to do when I was a girl.
I will wait.

THE BODY OF JESUS IS PLACED IN THE TOMB

—John 19: 40

"Lip of earth, take back your dust, wind. This is the part
you do not own."

None of us do. "He had to go and talk to the dead,
explain why He hid the sun in His pockets."

This was not the end. It had never been.

All the dead know as much, and that is why
they wait for Him. "They'll talk their talk—and He will
come back again, answer every question. He will
say what He is." That is why she does not move.

"Stars, see how they begin to speak. Birds gather gnats.

"It is a great drama, though I'm not sure how much of it exists.

"It did once."

Everything is half-baked, waiting, as his mother had always done.
The tune, half sung, she knew that, a song only she could hear.
La-la. In the face of a fear that devours,
she goes where she needs to, becomes His child.

She hums in the gloam, as if that will save her.
"Come back, Little One. Your mother knows—Your girl.

She will wait for as long as you like."

The Seven Sorrows and Seven Joys of St. Joseph

THE DOUBT THAT IS JOSEPH

"The labored turn, hand cupped low, beneath the curve;
it took that—virtue again asking: 'What do you know
of me, Joseph, the gilded?'

"You see, there's comfort in always being wrong.

"(Even the nothing I know—not enough.)

"Distance had been the rightness to it: the first bride,
offered, farthest from the grip and turns of this world.
She moved among birds. I don't say this as a youth,
but as one who's seen heaven, hidden. She is
too mild for flaw; too right, too alone.

"So my first thought was Roman, or local.
Like some David, warrior, I sidled younger men—
though with what power?

"But no, she was still the untouchable, almost reclusive,
scorned because she lived beyond praise.

"Her mother grew grim, would not speak of it, or to me;
and so I grieved, wondered how I could lighten her load—
that wincing finally getting me. She wasn't
right with things, with what I knew or
could be made to understand.

"And so I carried my own other—as the spit turned:
Mary, my teacher, answering a world beyond us both."

THE POVERTY OF JESUS' BIRTH

"The swaddling vestiges of donkey, a crib stained
with grainy drool. Leave off with what you know! There is
no place for you beyond the place you occupy. You are
function and design. Even your name—a given.

"'Give it up, always,' God says. Food, too, is a fiction, and hunger!
Babes and pregnant women, my too personal sense of justice.

"He needs you for—exactly—nothing!

"And so nothing must walk around in this shell, doing
what the virtuous seem to.

"And the truth is, I'm happy to do that much: it gives me reason, seasons.
What have any of us ever had but that? What will any of us ever have?

"A baby, a wife, a man not especially needed.

"Praise God for the Truth He is, for the One He is. Praise God
for each lie I need to tell me about myself, for its wane—
as I fight my secret, important way."

THE CIRCUMCISION

—Luke 2: 21

"So we are all welcomed: men, into the human family—
the blood that spills us, that we must spill.

"Life is beyond us, little one: our small roles, the worlds
we fashion. It is a blessing that He breaks in to take precedence,
the One who would see us dance!

"In our pain, yes: in our final agonies, but in the joy that owns us
as well. We will dance, carry you over our heads
because our time here is brief. So though you won't remember this
or the pain, little man, know that it will remember you,
as it has remembered all who have come before—what would,
even now, take us: the chosen, Messiah to the nations.

"We are the breath of God blowing down the ages, leveling peoples
before us! His doing, do not forget that. We are Jews, and our history
will always be marked with our blood.

"It will take you in sorrow, little man, as it will take me.
So let our agony be the praise it is as well; let us speak out of
more than pain when our time comes.

"It is His song we move."

THE PROPHECY OF SIMEON

—Luke: 2: 25–35

"Her suffering has always been quietly beyond me:
the barest ripple across her face—each like a breeze over water.
Her spaces deepen while I pose, a feint in the direction
of strength I do not possess.

"I've learned to sit close by, like a shepherd, staff along side,
close enough to accept correction—the ancient voices which move her.
I do what men do: fetch wood, move furniture, try to be a place
she can count on. But I cannot reach her.

"She likes my jokes, because they amuse me.

"When she sighs, my soul deepens, shifts like shelves of rock.
This prophecy is like that. What does it portend?
Whose heart moves in hers, what sorrow? Is she God's breastplate,
the only candle in that wind?

"This temple is too much for me—and my kin.

"She is wife, yes, always, but more, because she is a white room
I move in: a speech already written, a yes.

"I walk alongside, alone in my folly."

THE FLIGHT INTO EGYPT

—Matthew 2: 13–15

    "I had no sense of what I was doing in Israel.
    My world, given over to foreign places, to speech I cannot hear.

    "It's hard not to look at all of this as metaphor.

    "And how will I find work? Gather where workers will, help
    with free advice, motion for food when the time comes?
    My place will arrive, more slowly than sustenance.

    "Mary and Jesus will know hunger again—and I will feel indicted.

    "She will not care, of course, does not now. We could die,
    and she would not change, accepting leaves as they blow off trees,
    any wind, all of them foreign, and so home to her in some way.

    "The place-holder must hold down his place!
    He must do what's been given, eat the food of beggars
    until everything wrong in him dies.

    "I will do what I am told.

    "(Self-pity lives everywhere, comes with its long face, tongue—
    all lies want to matter!)

    "So let me respect God at least, the furrow he widens!

"I am happy to serve in any capacity. I am every father in every family. I am the bugs and the beasts, a summer pool and the twilight which follows the day.

"So we continue this walk, hearing only the sounds we choose to make—meeting every turn, into new demands. Towns come up. People trade, sometimes give for help given.
I will be disrupted at every turn, made uncomfortable, brought to pain, because I thought I knew something once,

because I still do."

THE RETURN FROM EGYPT

—Matthew 2: 19–23

"Dreams still tap, cane me through the dark;
they say Galilee: Nazareth—more alien soil. Still, who am I to deny
what moves us? How else can God lead the blind, the deaf?
I am not a flower of the most high like Mary is, her petals
so soaked in Light that each fiber names itself.

"I grow to appreciate darkness, slowly. Her equanimity leads us.

"Go create a home, nights say, one which cannot be made.
Still, we've done this before: I work for free, people notice;
crumbs will be our delight; then trading, never asking for the price.

"But the present always feeds its birds—

"our Child, too young for speech, looking at me
until all I know begins to wither, until my soul takes its meaning.

"Even on my lap He draws me, painfully, out of myself.
Soon it will be go this way, saw that. New ways will open,
new probabilities in wood. My inclinations will accost—
which can only help. Each interaction takes something:
my sense of who I am, my face in the water.
I can't lift the boy without feeling a grimace of wrongs.

"The fool and his ways—let them be parted.

"There is no foreseeable end to it, not on this side.
My Son has opened the wound that will, should, never close.
Each urge names me more surely than my parents. I feel them
both more often now, close by, take joy in that,
because I am their short-comings.

"My sins save my life."

THE LOSS OF THE CHILD JESUS

—Luke 2: 41–52

    The laughter, his brothers, are a river—.
    These are the faces that have made him. After all, if he's learned
    anything, it's not to move beyond his sight.

    But that, as it turns, is wrong as well. And so, rattled out
    of a false peace, he takes his place, foraging through time
    and time again. He has to look for the Boy who is never lost.

    None of it makes sense—which does.

    Never much to begin with, Joseph has grown lesser
    with the years, as his Son gives light to the moon, the trees:
    Dad is a peripheral witness, Mercy's toad, an orange pollen dust.

    He works under his Son's gaze, knows now that nothing good
    can come from this new widening: Rabbis
    who won't suffer Him because He knows them, clearly,
    each in turn.
                But how else could this world be changed?
    Joseph too, if it be his lot to manage that pace?

    This loss—losing his Son to the public, will be permanent,
    his own job, done, or nearly so; which, again, makes sense,
    since he can only help build the stage.

    Soon it will be his last table, chair.

But the Boy, he must change the world. It is the reach
He was born for: carnage—the unquenchable thirst of God.

Gospel Sonnets

THROUGH BEELZEBUB

(Matthew 12: 22–32)

    He offered the Pharisees the only way:
    without one—in the span of a healing hand.
    But profs are so used to games, to a me-first sway
    of logic that no other world can stand.

    "Your mind is no place to live! It's a house without
    a door or room, an Escher stair—without friends.
    Why not come clean? Each dawn arrives at about
    the same time! Each day opens roses, the throats of wrens.
    What nature gleams under your dominion, sun?
    So shape your words to Truth! You'll find your voice
    in its wake: new words will make your seasons run—
    shoals of fish will split in discord, remake each choice.

    "Know life by the joy it brings. That's why I plumb.
    Like a fife, I play you—in tones to make kingdoms come."

A TREE AND ITS FRUITS

(Matthew 12: 33–37)

>Here a man is his word: the Old West, Belle's knell,
>Jerusalem-style; before personal baggage, before
>psychological gods or their empty hell;
>when the wages of sin offered less than a candy store.
>But the world has always spoken well of lies,
>and Pharisees gather still where they always have:
>among constituents, to cut up a pie—
>its creased tin: holy poverty's only salve.
>
>Either deeds matter or they don't. Each rings
>a tree: the extent of our yeses, of our delay.
>These must come first. Only the muddied can sing—
>each just another liar-along-the-way.
>
>We cannot count our fruit, on the passing of years.
>The number is heaven's; each toast, for a king in arrears.

THE PHARISEES WOULD BE A SIGN

(Matthew 12: 38–42)

> The precise, abstracted, are unconvinced. This shtick,
> this urgent voice would awake the new—in bling!
> They'd caught his act before: a practiced trick
> of light; and the depths that commentary brings,
> gone. . . . But he chooses not to play, this cock:
> "You fools love boredom, though it is never enough!
> Tell me, what ship unloads before it docks?
> Let Jonah, baptized, teach you to swim through your rough
> repose. And know that Nineveh will reject
> each lie you invent because your Answer walks here.
> And Sheba! Did you expect your insistent defects
> would earn her respect. I am King Solomon's sear. . . .
>
> "You don't have to hire a dog to find a sign.
> You have one, aren't, in space or numbered time."

THE RETURN OF THE UNCLEAN SPIRIT

(Matthew 12: 43–45)

>Without nutrients, any blood on which to feed,
>the leech returns to a pool that he creates.
>(His un-friend, gone, he has no flesh to read,
>no memories to turn, no stories, no hate.)
>Bored, he morphs into man, invents a clean,
>well-lighted place—complete with black balloons—
>where he can drink, until the Hemingway scene
>loses its youth. His fancy, twice a boon,
>indicts itself, outside of record time.
>So he comes back: potato chips in the crease
>of the couch, a smashed TV. He invents the dime,
>calls for a misery of broken police.
>
>No need to look for a final, fatal turn.
>The seed is always there: the need, the burn.

St. Anthony Speaks

(FROM THE MIRACLES OF ST. ANTHONY—

whose chapter headings are ignored by the saint as he chooses, rather, a more direct discourse)

THE PRESENTATION MADE BY ST. ANTHONY TO PEOPLE WHO SPOKE VARIOUS DIFFERENT LANGUAGES

Fernando, we walk our knees—
don't hide in hiddenness,
in off art, in Our Lady's cuff.
We need you to read the braille
of our rainy skulls.

What did your left hand look like,
rising up off a table? Was there
a delicacy in the pad below the thumb,
a film over the thin soup you shared?

Let us sit in a corner.

"Very well . . . I will join you
on the floor.

"It's really quite simple, you know:
I had nothing to add—so I didn't.

"I laughed like you,
sometimes enjoyed the joke
for a moment too long, the echo
of what brought it forth.
I liked that.
But who has not done the same thing?

"I liked to hear the birds, as you do.

"Mountain air exhilarated.

"I kicked stones up there, flicked them
forward with brothers
to see who could get more lift, distance.

"But what you want what you already have.

"People heard different languages
because I only spoke one.

"Nothing else seemed worth its time
or place.

"Don't worry. Live in God's house—
this moment: rainbows in beveled glass,
the slow wonder in a blown bottle.

You can surf the flowers.

"Pastures of Church—I knew places
as a boy, where I could play mumbly-peg
with a friend, shout out
as loud as I wanted among the trees."

ST. ANTHONY PREACHES TO THE FISH

"I have always enjoyed them,
the fish.

Some of my best friends . . .

"You wonder: what can *you* do?
(God-fish, you fish.) But see,
your voice will be God's,
speaking the truth that becomes,
that gilds this world.

"Even when the Cathars heard,
after all, who knew what they got?
It's the projection that matters, the hope,
particles so pure that
science can't neuter them.

"Go ahead. Announce your yawp
over the rooftops of the world!

"No one will listen!

"Not that it matters.
(No one notices the dwarves either:
their freshly baked bread, their beer,
how they bumble into song.

"Pull out an extra log on the lawn

for your friends. Let the fire,
the ascending embers speak to,
create the early stars.)

"Here's the idea:
you must always take things further—
past what you know. Until your life's
just you, expecting, always on the cusp
of something entirely new."

HOW HE WAS SEEN SIMULTANEOUSLY IN TWO PLACES

"I had so much personality
I needed to be in two places at once!

"Jesus answered, and I was both
here and there—like everybody.
(There was just so much of me
to go around!)

"Let the world befoul a name
you do not have. What flourish
would recommend you, after all?
What badge could you wear?

"St. Paul was all things to all people
because he was nothing to himself.

"I tried not to defend myself
in the public of my mind. This life
has never been about enumerations, has it,
a spread of roses?

"So go ahead, smear your canvas.

"You will be mercy's next face:
cubist, but warm."

ST. ANTHONY ASSISTS A MONK WHO WAS TEMPTED SEXUALLY

"I gave him the sweater
to cover himself—to take his mind
and put it somewhere else.

"And that's always the problem, isn't it?

"I didn't make or remake myself, ever—
none of us do, whatever your world claims!
I did nothing—but that.
I was wax, an impression, a pocket full of change.

"It was not an easy thing for that friar:
his nature thrown in his face.

"Good—but not easy!

"Jesus allows the fool to meet himself
at every turn.

"Eventually the two become friends.
Just you and the mirror.

"Look! The good has wrinkles!"

HE REPLACES A WOMAN'S HAIR THAT HAD BEEN TORN OFF HER HEAD

"Women are a great good—
like the morning: this one, both
in drawing our feet up from the dirt,
and in her need
to recover that beautiful hair!

"Be patient
with what you cannot understand!

"Count yourself graced
to be in the presence of a new day,
when all things are outlined,
given shape, when new possibilities
are made clear. This is what she gives.
Receive, receive.
What could be bad here?

"You lose nothing except a false notion:
your import, place in the world.

"This is why we all have to learn to work
in silence, next to her, as Joseph did.

"There will be corrections for you
to make, calculations, revisions.
(These will keep you involved.)

But do so quietly,
with the other in mind."

HE REVEALS ONE OF SATAN'S TRICKS TO THE FRIARS

"It's a sorry tale: the disturbed
fashion plate, always on about something:
gyrating over here, each limb
contending with the others.

"For God's sake, don't make the mistake
of dancing with him!

"He is much larger than you
and abides by no rule.

"Let simplicity, Jesus, speak your name.
Let that be your answer to his wheedling.
It's a perfect discourse
because it offers none.

"It's a world ours cannot recognize.
Take your lunch there, on tree's
midfoot; you can stretch your legs,
enjoy each moss's slow reach,
the high turn of the leaves.

"Giant money will always have
center stage, bigger teams—
because it makes so much noise.

"You will be over here,
a citizen of what matters.

"I like to think of it as baseball again, in 1889:
the long baggy pants, everybody
choking up on bottle-necked bats,
everybody named Pee Wee—on deck,
chawing for all they're worth,
solicitations to soiled wood."

"His shows are just want
without means—for the incorporeal,
all he cannot have.

"He rages at who he has become."

HOW HE BOLDLY PREACHED AGAINST VICES

"Life is its own custard;
everyone who has ever walked
under green leaves,
dappling sun knows that!

"Take an apple.
Rinsed, it is all it can be,
no better than the tree it came from
or the sky, to be sure,
but great and fat in its goodness:
integral, a part of heaven, talking.

"The bees buzz for you.

"Why live anywhere else?

"But this ridiculous
invented good, this rioting need to rule,
to invent a life as suitable throne?

"Privilege is a road
paved with stones not here.
It is the voice of no one, singing.

"So, consider the green
beneath the summer flower,
and then consider it again."

HOW A DOWNPOUR DID NOT DAMPEN HIS LISTENERS

"The miracle was in the language,
not in what followed.
The horse makes the cart so,
does it not? Otherwise
it's just a country basket!

"This is how heaven has always come—
in the hearing: think of a quart of oil,
pouring, puckering the plastic container,
think of that liquid, reflecting the sun.

"What could be more eloquent?

"So many cling to vestiges.
Miracles are the norm;
this does not seem to occur to people.

"Build Him a little bird house early
tomorrow morning. Twitter, sing
as you do. (Your province is so small
that the voice won't even be yours.)

"And do not fret.
You have already changed the world."

THE ANGELIC POSTMAN

"He knocks, but they never hear,
weighted down as he is with packages;
off then, little wings on his cap.
It's not an easy job, I imagine,
or an especially rewarding one.
I mean it's not like he gets to be there
when they open the thing: the confetti,
champagne, the complicated handshakes.

"All of that is for others.

"No, he's gone, about his business.
His job is barking dogs, spiritual biscuits
that won't quite hold together.
And ethereal transit, that can't be fun.
Where you need to be you are, almost
before you can think it: the predictable,
slight tremor each time before it happens.

"Everybody's got their complaints, of course;
everybody has their mundane place
in the grand design. He didn't want
his job. He didn't ask for it, but what
is he gonna do? He keeps thinking
retirement is going to set things straight—
once this idea of job satisfaction
has finally been delivered, put to rest,
along with the terrible suit."

Notes

THE PAPAL SASH

The final image from Billy Collins's poem "Catholicism."

WE DID SAY A ROSARY IN THE CAR—

Jude's programs are funded by West Virginia. As is mentioned in the next poem, he has Down's. (He says he's allergic to it.)

SAGRADA FAMILIA

My family and I got to spend a semester in Gaming, Austria, teaching at FUS's European campus.

I USE A TINY BOWL FOR CEREAL

Many postmodernist poets dismiss the whole idea of symbol, since that would imply order or meaning beneath things.

It's a Wonderful Life is a classic movie, produced shortly after WWII—when national gratitude was in full swing. Clarence, the clumsy angel, notes that when a bell rings, an angel has gotten his or her wings.

YEATS, ONCE A RAVEN, HAYSTACK

"Cuchulain Comforted" is one of Yeats's last poems: a Danteesque bit of repentance I think. The dance, I imagine, occurs later.

Notes

PAT'S FACE TINTS

The two mentioned popular songs are part of the corny idealism of early rock and roll: "Where oh where can my baby be./The Lord took her away from me./She's gone to heaven, so I've got to be good;/so I can see my baby when I leave-a this world."

MY BROTHER LARRY FIGHTS A ROTTWEILER

The phrase "if you don't count personal issues" is a comic lift from a Wallace Stevens video. His old friend, a Mr. Brown, insists that Wallace was a happy man if you didn't include his personal life.

PIX'S HORSE

"A nice set" is a lift from *The Waste Land*.

TWELVE-CUSTOMER PAPER ROUTE

"Made in Japan" meant something made cheaply in those days, easily breakable; because you couldn't afford something better.
    "The end of the world" was a Skeeter Davis pop song which lamented the great pangs of adolescent parting, a reservoir of angst—nicely available for an eleven year old.
    "Winter covering us" is a lift from Eliot's *The Waste Land*.
    "Bend to it again" is a lift from Kerouac's *On the Road*.

BIRTHDAY POEM

The quoted matter at end is taken from Eliot's lineage in "East Coker."

WHEN THE KIDS WERE BORN

Bowling shoes have a used feel to them when you put them on. You can almost feel all the feet who were there before you: a big party! (Creepy, as they say.) And so it was with the sleeping chair at the hospital.

Notes

OUR LADY APPEARS SO OFTEN THESE DAYS

The last line is lifted from *Galaxy Quest*, one of my favorite Sam Rockwell movies.

WE INVENTED CHOCOLATE MILK

There was a company, don't know if it still exists, which at one time would sell you an unnamed star. With proof of purchase you could name it anything you liked.

"A TURTLE IS CONSIDERED OBESE IF IT IS TOO CHUBBY TO WITHDRAW INTO ITS SHELL"

Both the holes and the Albert Hall were lifted from a Beatles' song: "Day in the Life"

SO MUCH LIGHT GREEN ENCROACHES

Robert Young starred as Jim Anderson in *Father Knows Best*, a t.v. series which ran from 1954-1963. Not a favorite of Walker Percy.

THE RETURN OF THE UNCLEAN SPIRIT

(Matthew 12: 43-45)

"A Clean Well-Lighted Place" is a Hemingway short story.

THE PRESENTATION MADE BY ST. ANTHONY TO PEOPLE WHO SPOKE VARIOUS DIFFERENT LANGUAGES

St. Anthony responds to the speaker's concern about his missing person in hagiographic lore, choosing to completely shift the loci of these poems. They don't really concern themselves with the original medieval sources much—though the saint does upon occasion make an oblique reference to them.

Anthony's given name was Fernando Martins de Bulhões.

Notes

ST. ANTHONY PREACHED TO THE FISH

Anthony spent much of his time preaching to the Cathars, a Manichean sect who wanted to trample the body underfoot—beneath spiritual shoes (one guesses). In this particular tale, he couldn't get them to listen and so turned to the fish who, as it turned out, had much more sense.

HOW HE WAS SEEN SIMULTANEOUSLY IN TWO PLACES

The saint, in his great wisdom, praises modern art.

HE REVEALS ONE OF SATAN'S TRICKS TO THE FRIARS

In this story Satan harasses the brothers by carrying on, tearing up a wheat field. St. Anthony teaches them to recollect themselves—and everything is as it's always been the next morning, good.

THE ANGELIC POSTMAN

Basically an angel mails a letter for the saint in the original text. It seemed unfortunate that he did not get any further play in the proceedings.

Acknowledgments

"After Simeon," *America*.

"At the West Virginia Dept. of Motor Vehicles," "Our Lady Appears so often these days," "There is a hollow in winter," *St. Katherine's Review*.

"I found this old entry about my son," *Lipton Poetry Review*.

"Mary Receiving the Pierced Body," *Christianity and Literature*.

"So much green light encroaches," *Anglican Theological Review*.

"The Prophecy of Simeon," *The Heavenly Country*," ed. by M. Martin.

www.ingramcontent.com/pod-product-compliance
Lightning Source LLC
Chambersburg PA
CBHW071440160426
43195CB00013B/1972